Sea Riddles

Written by Angus Phelps

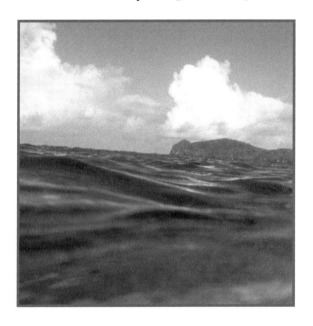

Celebration Press

Parsippany, New Jersey

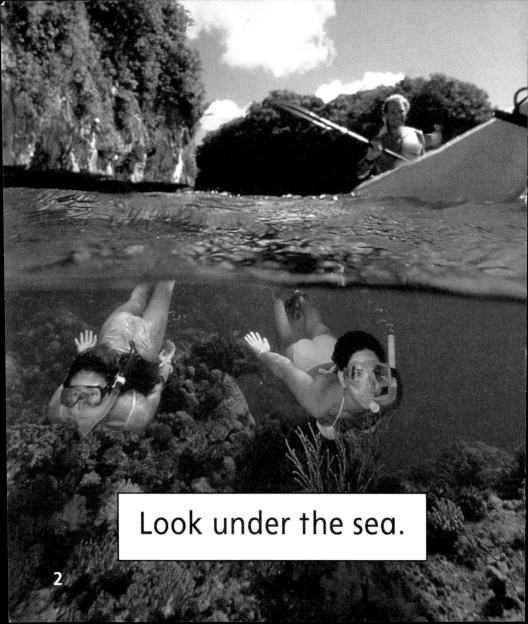

Look under the sea.

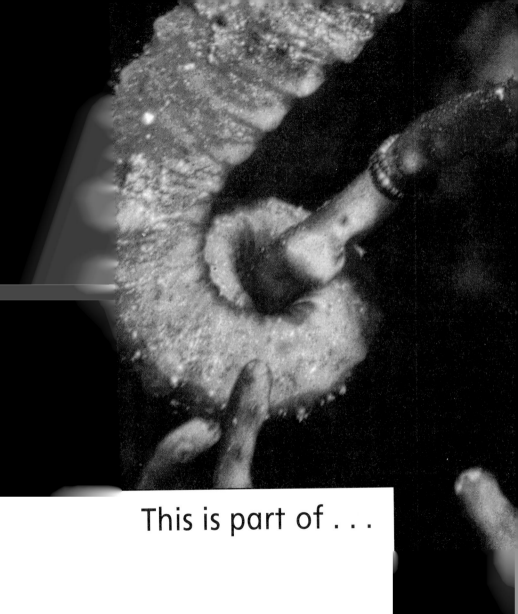

This is part of . . .

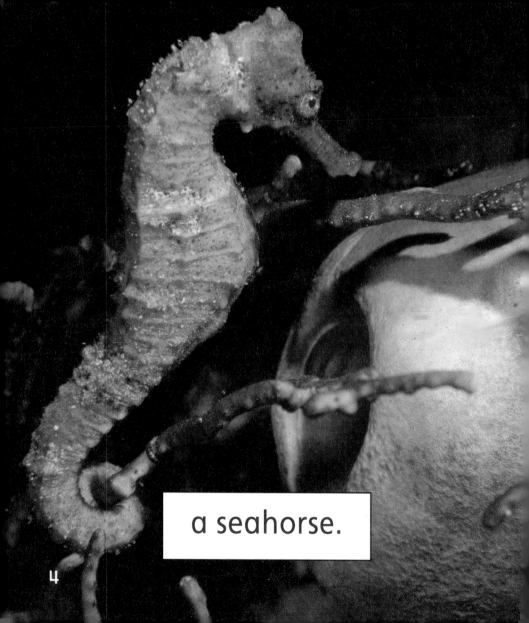

a seahorse.

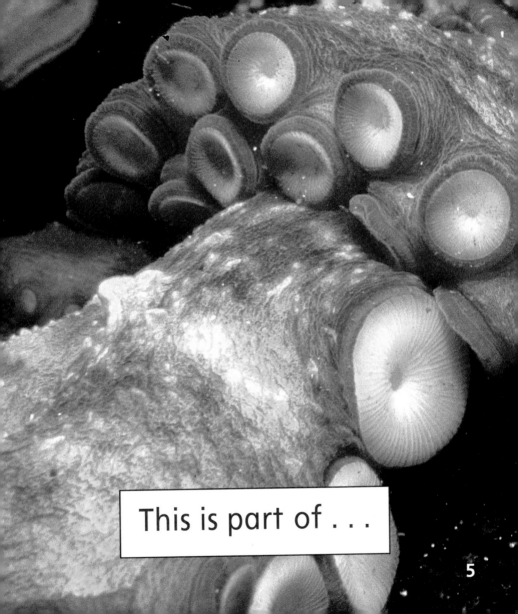

This is part of . . .

5

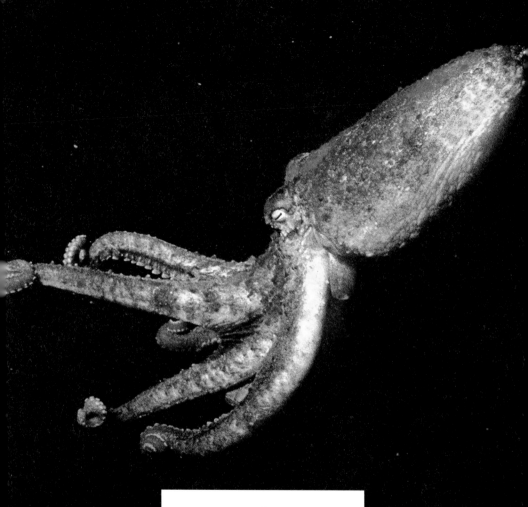

an octopus.

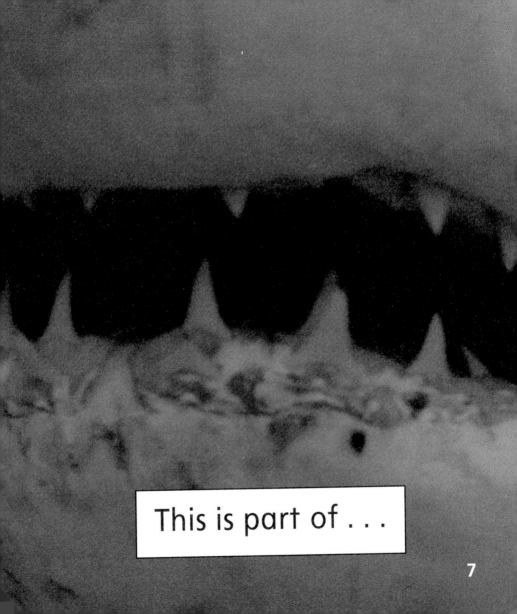

This is part of . . .

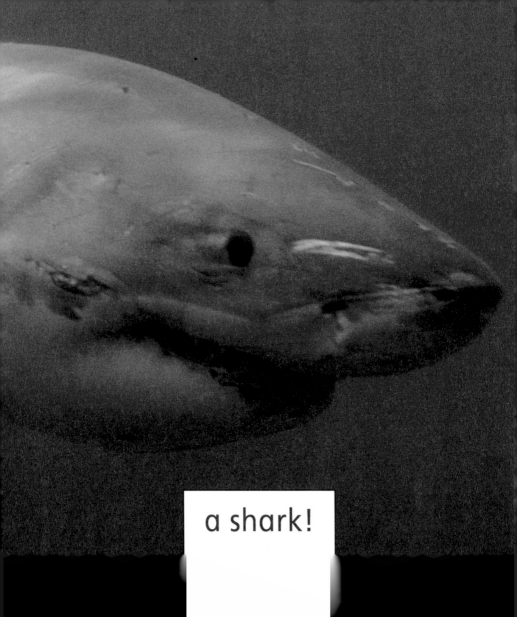

a shark!